GET READY FOR SOME COOL CRITTERS!

This book is full of rad reptiles like lizards and crocodiles. You'll also learn about some animals that are not reptiles, like frogs and salamanders.

Turn the page to meet them!

WHAT ARE REPTILES?

Reptiles are animals that have a backbone and dry, scaly skin. Snakes, lizards, turtles, and crocodiles are all kinds of reptiles.

Reptiles can't stay warm on their own. They need to move to a sunny spot to warm up.

Reptiles are covered in a special kind of skin called *scales*. The scales connect in a "sheet," and sometimes part of their skin can flake off. Not to worry—this is normal for them!

Turtles are covered in scales too. Their shells are made of bones and scales.

GREEN IGUANA

The green iguana has spikes on its neck, back, and on the upper part of its tail.

The green iguana is a scaly lizard that lives in trees in the rain forest.

They have sharp teeth and strong tails that they use to stay safe. They can also break off their tails if they are caught!

Green iguanas can sometimes be brown or black. They can even change to bright orange or gold at different times of the year.

PANTHER CHAMELEON

Panther chameleons change colors based on how they are feeling.

💡 **FAST FACTS**

Length
9–18 inches
(22.9–45.7 cm)

Weight
2.8–5.6 ounces
(79.4–158.8 g)

Chameleons can move their eyes in two different directions.

Panther chameleons come in lots of colors, from blue-green to red to orange, and even bright pink!

These lizards live in trees close to rivers and roads. They have special feet that hold on tight to tree branches. They use their long tongues to catch bugs.

KOMODO DRAGON

Komodo dragons are the biggest and heaviest lizards in the world.

FAST FACTS

Length
10 feet (3 m)

Weight
330 pounds
(150 kg)

Komodo dragon bites are deadly. This lizard has special spit called *venom* that comes out when it bites down.

with the Komodo dragon!

They wait and hide, and then catch an animal to eat with their sharp claws and teeth. Their teeth are big and jagged like steak knives! But their teeth are hidden by their thick gums.

AFRICAN BUSH VIPER

African bush vipers are snakes with spiky scales and bright colors.

These snakes can be found in shades of red, orange, gray, yellow, black, blue, and brown.

African bush vipers are so cool, they almost look like small dragons! They mostly live up in trees in rain forests.

African bush vipers eat mice, rats, and sometimes birds. They sit on tree branches at night, waiting for an animal to come near. Then the snake attacks!

BRAZILIAN RAINBOW BOA

The Brazilian rainbow boa is one of the prettiest snakes in the world.

FAST FACTS

Length
4–6 feet
(1.2–1.8 m)

Weight
2–3 pounds
(0.9–1.4 kg)

Brazilian rainbow boas are good swimmers.

Brazilian rainbow boas have tiny ridges on their scales. The ridges make light bounce off the scales. This gives the snake a rainbow shine!

These snakes are in the "boa" family. Boas hunt by slowly squeezing another animal until it stops moving.

AMERICAN CROCODILE

American crocodiles are large reptiles with rough, bumpy skin and wide jaws.

FAST FACTS

Length
Up to 15 feet
(4.6 m)

Weight
Up to
2,000 pounds
(907.2 kg)

If a crocodile gets too warm, it will open its mouth to cool down.

American crocodiles can be found near the sea, and in ponds and swamps.

They may look big and scary, but crocodiles are also shy. They like to be left alone.

EASTERN BOX TURTLE

Eastern box turtles are some of the most common turtles you can find outdoors.

The shell on an Eastern box turtle can grow back if it gets damaged.

The Eastern box turtle has a round shell that covers most of its body. These turtles are dark brown with yellow or orange markings.

The markings on the shell can blend in with leaves on the forest floor. This helps the turtle hide.

LOGGERHEAD TURTLE

Loggerhead turtles are named for their big heads.

Loggerhead turtles use their strong jaws to chomp on clams and sea urchins.

The loggerhead turtle is a kind of sea turtle. It has flippers instead of legs. It lives in the ocean most of the time.

Sea turtles have to swim to the top of the ocean to breathe air. They come to the land when it is time to lay eggs. When the babies hatch, they crawl back to the ocean.

GIANT TORTOISE

There are only two groups of giant tortoises and they both live on islands.

Giant tortoises
can live to be
more than 100
years old!

The giant tortoise has a big, round shell on its back. It likes to eat grass, leaves, fruit, and cactus.

Giant tortoises weigh more than most adult humans, but move very slowly. They also spend about 16 hours a day napping.

AMPHIBIANS

Frogs, toads, and salamanders may look like reptiles, but they are amphibians. There are important differences between reptiles and amphibians.

Frogs, toads, and salamanders can breathe and take in water through their skin.

These animals have thin skin with no scales. They live in the water when they are babies.

When they grow up, most of them move to land.

POISON FROG

Poison frogs come in bright colors: red, yellow, gold, green, and blue.

Length
0.4–2.4 inches
(0.1–6.1 cm)

Weight
0.02–0.14 ounces
(0.6–4 g)

Some poison frogs carry their babies on their back.

Poison frogs get their name from the poison in their skin. They get the poison from eating bugs that have eaten deadly plants.

The frog's colors warn other animals to stay away. If an animal eats the frog, it will become very sick.

COMMON TOAD

Common toads are found all over Britain, and on many islands in the United Kingdom.

FAST FACTS

Length
3–5 inches
(7.6–12.7 cm)

Weight
Up to 3 ounces
(85 g)

Common toads taste bad to other animals because of the poison on their skin.

This is a common toad.
Toads may look like frogs, but they are different. Toads have dry skin with warts, and they walk or hop on short legs. They live in fields and grasslands.

Common toads hunt at night. They like to eat slugs, spiders, worms, bugs, and ants.

FIRE SALAMANDER

Fire salamanders are black with orange or yellow markings.

FAST FACTS

Length
6–12 inches
(15.2–30.5 cm)
Weight
0.67 ounces
(19 g)

The name *salamander* comes from an Arabic word that means "lives in fire."

Fire salamanders are shy animals. They spend most of their time hiding under logs and rocks in the forest.

But don't get too close if you see one! These salamanders can squirt poison up to 1 foot (0.3 m) away.

AXOLOTL

Axolotls can only be found in two lakes near Mexico City, Mexico.

FAST FACTS

Length
6–18 inches
(15.2–45.7 cm)

Weight
2–8 ounces
(56.7–226.8 g)

Axolotls can regrow parts of their body if they get injured.

Axolotls look like baby salamanders, even as adults. They have webbed feet, gills, and a tail, and they live in the water.

They are usually a grayish-brown color, but they can turn lighter if they need to blend in.

Thank you for reading about so many cool reptiles and amphibians of the world. We hope you had fun meeting them!

METRIC TABLE

The metric system is a system of measurements. It is used in many parts of the world. It is also used by all scientists, no matter where they live. Here are some common abbreviations for metric measurements used in this book.

cm = centimeters (1 centimeter = .4 inch)

g = grams (1 gram = .03 ounce)

kg = kilograms (1 = 2.2 pounds)

m = meters (1 meter = 3.3 feet)